my itty-bitty bio

Wayne Gretzky

Cherry Lake Press

Published in the United States of America by Cherry Lake Publishing
Ann Arbor, Michigan
www.cherrylakepublishing.com

Reading Adviser: Marla Conn, MS, Ed., Literacy specialist, Read-Ability, Inc.
Book Designer: Jennifer Wahi
Illustrator: Jeff Bane

Photo Credits: © Allard One/Shutterstock, 5; © Click Images/Shutterstock, 7; © Jerry Coli/Dreamstime.com, 9, 21; © Ned Yeung/Dreamstime.com, 11, 22; © alarico/Shutterstock, 13; © Michael Bush/Dreamstime.com, 15, 23; © Kathy Hutchins/Shutterstock, 17; © DardaInna/Shutterstock, 19; Cover, 1, 12, 14, 16, Jeff Bane; Various frames throughout, © Shutterstock images

Cherry Lake Press is an imprint of Cherry Lake Publishing Group.

Library of Congress Cataloging-in-Publication Data

Names: Pincus, Meeg, author. | Bane, Jeff, 1957- illustrator.
Title: Wayne Gretzky / Meeg Pincus ; illustrated by Jeff Bane.
Description: Ann Arbor, Michigan : Cherry Lake Publishing, 2021. | Series: My itty-bitty bio | Includes index. | Audience: Grades K-1
Identifiers: LCCN 2020005718 (print) | LCCN 2020005719 (ebook) | ISBN 9781534168435 (hardcover) | ISBN 9781534170117 (paperback) | ISBN 9781534171954 (pdf) | ISBN 9781534173798 (ebook)
Subjects: LCSH: Gretzky, Wayne, 1961---Juvenile literature. | Hockey players--Canada--Biography--Juvenile literature.
Classification: LCC GV848.5.G73 P56 2021 (print) | LCC GV848.5.G73 (ebook) | DDC 796.962092 [B]--dc23
LC record available at https://lccn.loc.gov/2020005718
LC ebook record available at https://lccn.loc.gov/2020005719

Printed in the United States of America
Corporate Graphics

table of contents

About the author: Meeg Pincus has been a writer, editor, and educator for 25 years. She loves to write inspiring stories for kids about people, animals, and our planet. She lives near San Diego, California, where she enjoys the beach, reading, singing, and her family.

About the illustrator: Jeff Bane and his two business partners own a studio along the American River in Folsom, California, home of the 1849 Gold Rush. When Jeff's not sketching or illustrating for clients, he's either swimming or kayaking in the river to relax.

my story

I was born in Ontario, Canada.
It was 1961.

I have a younger sister and three younger brothers.

I learned to play hockey when I was 2. I played with 10-year-olds when I was only 6.

I only scored one goal my first **season**. This made me work harder.

I became one of the best hockey players. My **nickname** is "The Great One."

What do you want to be
when you grow up?

I scored 1,000 goals by age 13. At 17, I signed with a **professional** hockey team. I played for 21 seasons.

Coca-Cola
Rexall
AIR CANADA
Bell
PRONGER
25
HUSKINS
40
44
PAHLSSON
26

I won many awards. I scored the most goals and most **assists** in hockey history.

I **retired**. My hockey number retired too! This means no one else in the **NHL** can use my number. This is a great honor.

I am a family man. I love my wife and our five children. I am proud of my family.

What are you most proud of?

I started a **foundation**. It helps kids in need play hockey.

I am a hockey **legend**. I try to give back what hockey gave me.

What would you want to ask me?

timeline

1978

1960

Born
1961

1999

2060

glossary

assists (uh-SISTS) in hockey, the acts of a player helping another player to score

foundation (foun-DAY-shuhn) an organization that gives money to important causes

legend (LEJ-uhnd) someone who is famous or well-known for something

NHL (EN AYCH EL) National Hockey League

nickname (NIK-name) a name for a person that others use instead of the person's real name

professional (pruh-FESH-uh-nuhl) making money for working hard at something others do for fun

retired (rih-TIRED) stopped working or playing a sport

season (SEE-zuhn) a part of the year when a certain sport or activity takes place

index